Cairo in 3 Days:

The Definitive Tourist Guide Book That Helps You Travel Smart and Save Time

Finest City Guides

Book Description

This guide fills an important niche for business and personal travelers who wish to visit Cairo, but are limited by time. It will help you to organize your trip and enjoy your visit. We've gathered information from Cairo entrepreneurs and expats alike, giving you the information you need to have the most fun in your 3-day visit to Cairo – filled as it will be with a variety of leisure and cultural pursuits.

Within this book, we'll fill the need for knowledge of the city, before you ever step on the plane that will take you there. Read all about their currency and local customs, so you can hit the ground running.

We'll show you the best of all there is to see and do in Cairo, from the world-renowned, must-see pyramids to the other historic sites and the museums. We also provide a guide to the best places to stay and eat, in all price ranges, while you're there.

The People of Cairo

The people of Cairo are largely very helpful and friendly. While the Bedouin people live in Sinai and the deserts of Egypt, most of the Egyptians you meet in town work in factories or companies. They largely dress in western-style clothing. Most have graduated from university. They often speak good English and will happily help you if you ask.

Language

The official Egyptian language is Standard Arabic. However, the most spoken language is Egyptian Arabic. In addition to English, you'll also find people in Cairo who speak French, especially those who work in the business world.

Culinary Delights

Egyptian cuisine includes dishes like:

- Koshari, which is a mixture of pasta, rice, lentils & other ingredients
- Molokheyya, chopped, then cooked okra with coriander sauce and garlic
- Fel Medames, which is made from mashed fava beans

Fava beans are also used in the making of falafel, which was first made in Egypt and has since spread around to other areas of the Middle East.

The cuisine of Cairo shares many similarities with that of the entire Eastern Mediterranean area, including grape leaves and rice-stuffed vegetables, Kebab, baklava and Baba Ghannoug.

Holidays

Jan 1 - New Year's Day - Bank holiday

Jan 7 - Coptic Christmas Day - National holiday

Jan 25 - Revolution Day - National holiday

Apr 25 - Sinai Liberation Day - National holiday

Apr 29 - Coptic Good Friday - Observance

Apr 30 - Coptic Holy Saturday - Observance

May 1 - Coptic Easter Sunday - National holiday

May 1 - Labor Day - National holiday

May 2 - Spring Festival - National holiday

Jun 30 - June 30 Revolution - National holiday

Jul 1 - Bank Holiday - Bank holiday

Jul 7 - Eid el Fitr - National holiday

Jul 8 - End of Ramadan Day 2 - National holiday

Jul 9 - End of Ramadan Day 3 - National holiday

Jul 23 - Revolution Day - National holiday

Aug 15 - Flooding of the Nile - Observance

Sep 11 - Coptic New Year - Observance

Sep 13 - Feast of the Sacrifice - National holiday

Sep 14 - Feast of the Sacrifice Day 2 National holiday

Sep 15 - Feast of the Sacrifice Day 3 - National holiday

Sep 16 - Feast of the Sacrifice Day 4 - National holiday

Oct 3 - Muharram - National holiday

Oct 6 - Armed Forces Day - National holiday

Dec 12 - Prophet Mohammed's birthday - National holiday

Dec 21 - December Solstice - Season

Religious Beliefs

The majority of Cairo residents are Muslim. About 10% of the people in Egypt are Christians. Most of these are worshipers in the Coptic Orthodox Church. Coptic Christianity was Egypt's dominant religion, before an introduction of Islam.

Only approximately 200 Jewish people still live in Cairo. Most of the other Jews have emigrated to the US or Israel in the past 50 years.

You'll find many mosques in Cairo, from large to small. Muslims traditionally pray five times each day. At noon on Fridays, they gather for noon prayer. Many offices, businesses and schools are closed on Friday.

Here is a quick preview of what you will learn in this tourist guide:

- Helpful information about Cairo
- Flying into the city
- Transportation tips in town
- Why Cairo is such a vibrant tourist spot
- Information on luxury and budget accommodations and what you'll get for your money
- The currency used in Cairo
- Tourist attractions you should make time to see
- Other attractions for entertainment and culture
- Events that may be running during your stay
- Tips on the best places to eat & drink for all price points, whether you want simple fare, worldwide dishes or Egyptian flavor

Table of Contents

1. Introduction 1
2. Key Information about Cairo 5
3. Transport to and in Cairo 8
4. Accommodations 15
5. Sightseeing 22
6. Eat & Drink 26
7. Culture and Entertainment 32
8. Special Events in Cairo 38
9. Safety in Cairo 44
10. Conclusion 46

1. Introduction

Cairo is the largest city in Africa and the Arab world, and sits on the Nile River bank. In its 1000-year history, it was once the capital of Middle Ages Egyptian dynasties, then a colonial enclave for the British, before becoming the modern industrialized city it is today.

Cairo today is a vibrant nation's capital, a city filled with teeming businessmen and tourists. Its population density per square mile is one of the largest in the world. Even as Cairo struggles with environmental and social over-crowding effects, it is the dominant city in Egypt – culturally, politically and economically – and is a popular destination for tourists.

A Brief History of Cairo

In 641 A.D., the settlement of al-Fustat was founded in the area that now includes Cairo. It was an Arab military encampment. Under ruling Egyptian dynasties, it grew into the major port city of the region.

A new city was founded in 969 A.D. by an Islamic sect known as the Fatimids. This would eventually become Cairo. The Fatimids would become Egyptian rulers, in a dynasty that would last for 200 years. Cairo was their capital city.

The Crusaders were defeated in the 12th century by a Sunni Muslim named Saladin. He founded the Ayyubid dynasty and kept Cairo as its capital. The Mamluks, Turkish conquerors, eclipsed the Ayyubids and would rule Egypt until 1516 A.D. During this period, Cairo established a new university, and became a key city in the spice trade. This was the beginning of the vibrant, international city we know today.

Neighborhoods

Cairo has a number of districts or neighborhoods that vary in their social standards. Most people in the neighborhoods will welcome you.

Heliopolis (also called Masr el-Gedida) is similar to many US urban areas. They have bars, fancy restaurants, sports clubs, gyms and even a McDonald's. The traffic is bustling, and in Heliopolis, you won't see many women wearing skirts.

In Doqqi and Zamalek, you'll see women wearing skirts every day. Overall, the people are devout Muslims but do not necessarily practice some of the more strict traditions that are sometimes seen in other predominantly Muslim countries. Both Muslim and non-Muslim residents co-exist within Cairo.

What does Cairo Offer its Visitors?

You only need to look up at the Pyramid in the Cairo skyline to remember that the city's ancient places are more a part of the fabric of the city than they are exhibits for tourists.

Tourists have flocked to Cairo for thousands of years, and the Giza Pyramids and Sphinx are the most impressive and oldest of impressive attractions in our world. You might think that other Cairo attractions pale when compared to the pyramids. Actually, some of the most interesting Cairo sites are rare places where the people live their daily lives in ancient surroundings.

2. Key Information about Cairo

Money Matters

Egypt's currency is the Egyptian pound (LE). You don't need to exchange currency before you arrive, since the rate is better within Egypt. Most vendors also accept Sterling, Euros and dollars, but they only take these foreign currencies in notes - no coins.

Egyptian Notes are found in these values:
5, 10, 20, 50, 100 and 200 Le note

Coins are used in these denominations:
1 Le COIN
50 piastres coin (this equals one half of 1 Le)
25 piastres coin (this equals one quarter of 1 Le)

You will find your money goes further if you exchange it for Egyptian pounds. The best places to exchange money are banks and currency exchange shops, which are found everywhere. Don't change your money at restaurants or hotels, since you won't get the best exchange rate and will lose money that way.

Mastercard and Visa are welcomed at most restaurants and hotels. However, there are high processing fees, so businesses prefer cash. When you use your credit cards, you will usually be expected to pay the bank's processing fees.

ATMs are found outside banks and in major hotels. If you're worried about losing money, you can put money on your card and then draw it from ATMs in Cairo.

Tipping

Tipping is quite common in Egypt. It is done everywhere, including bars, coffee shops, restaurants, stores and even at gas stations. Many people count on tips for their livelihood, particularly people who work on cruise ships and in hotels.

Tips show appreciation, so it's left to you whether you want to tip for good service. Here are a few minimum amounts for tipping. (Note: Tipping for taxis is found in the taxi section.)

Hotel bellmen usually get about 5 Egyptian pounds per bag, at a minimum.

Housecleaning people in your hotel are usually tipped at a rate of about 10 Egyptian pounds per day.

Don't tip your drivers, wait staff or others with COINS of your home country. They don't have a way to change coins at their banks.

Restaurant Tipping

You don't need to figure your tip by the total bill amount, as you may be accustomed to doing. 5 Egyptian pounds per person at your table is the acceptable minimum. If you had especially good food or service, you can leave more.

3. Transport to and in Cairo

Getting to Cairo by Plane

Cairo International Airport (IATA) is the country's main international airport. It is Egypt's busiest airport and the primary hub for EgyptAir, among other carriers. It is found in Heliopolis, an area about 9 ½ miles northeast of downtown Cairo.

Getting to Cairo from the Airport

It can be a bit of a pain to get to downtown Cairo. White meter taxis are found at the airport terminals. Their fee is EGP 3.00 plus EGP 2.50/kilometer. Insist on your driver using the meter, and don't accept fixed prices, as these may be as high as double that of a metered ride.

You can sometimes share a cab with others if you're headed for downtown Cairo from the airport. Your hotel may also arrange transport, but there is usually a fee for this service. The average cab trip from the airport to downtown Cairo shouldn't be more than 50 to 60 EGP, or $6 to $8 USD.

The easiest way to get from the airport to the city is through a limousine service, and they have pickup points in front of the airport terminals. They have fixed prices, depending on where you're heading and the category of car you choose.

- Category A is for luxury limos
- Category B is for mini buses that carry up to seven passengers
- Category C is for midsize cars

Cairo Cabs

Solid white taxi cabs are modern and the drivers usually use the meters. They are air conditioned, and fueled by natural gas. It's usually cheaper to take one of these, and you can hail them from the street, in town, as well.

Yellow taxis are usually only available with a reservation. They may pick up fares on their way to a scheduled stop. Drivers can't smoke in these cabs.

The black and white taxis are older, and the most common to see. They also have the oldest drivers and they don't use meters. Try to have exact change after your driver tells you what the charge will be. Drivers only give change reluctantly.

Uber works quite well in Cairo, but only if you have a 3G connection on a smartphone. You don't have to negotiate prices or worry about overcharges. The Uber drivers usually speak English and these rides are cash-free. It's a very good choice over Cairo's hit and miss quality in their regular cabs.

Payment and Tipping for Taxi's

Most Egyptians don't state prices before your trip. Rather, you'll pay through the car window after you get out. Some drivers expect a tourist to pay more than their standard rates. Walk away if you aren't told what the fare will be. You should choose your taxi. Don't let drivers choose YOU.

If you have more than one person, cabbies will generally expect you to pay more. Negotiate the price before you get in. Drivers usually do not accept more than four people in their cabs. Cabs are also more expensive when used late at night.

Don't pay for cabs with large bills. Drivers may pretend not to have change, and they may even attempt to switch the note out for a smaller one, and then claim you only gave them the smaller amount.

Taxi Precautions

Don't travel in a taxi if the vehicle is not safe, or if your driver is operating the vehicle in a reckless manner. Watch out for unlit roads at night. If your driver won't slow down for your comfort, ask him to stop immediately and then leave the cab.

Cairo Rental Cars

Rental cars in Cairo are not necessary or recommended. The traffic is overwhelming, unless you know the city. Vehicle traffic is consistent, but not in any way that is official. Road signs, right of way and lanes are often not followed.

Traffic signals are seldom seen and even where they are found, they are usually ignored. There are usually not many places in Cairo to park a car, either.

Public Transport in Cairo

The Metro

The metro system in Cairo was the first in Africa, and its most extensive. While it is sleek and modern, the lines are somewhat limited in their scope. The flat rate is 1 LE for each trip.

If you want a ticket, be aware that they don't really wait in lines at the ticket window (or anywhere else). You have to be assertive to get a turn. You can buy multiple tickets at once, so you won't have to wait again.

Cairo's Metro system has its main stations in Maadi and Dokki. They do not have a time-table schedule, but they do have frequent departures.

Buses

The large public buses are blue, red and white. They cover the full city, and are generally crowded. However, you can choose air conditioned buses, where the trip is more comfortable, and there is no standing allowed. They are available for boarding at Cairo's main square.

Cairo also has smaller buses that or blue, red and white or white and orange. Women traveling in Cairo are advised to take only the smaller buses, because of some problems with harassment of women.

You can hail a bus at street level. Shout out your destination and the driver of the bus going that way will stop for you.

If you plan to ride the bus later at night, note that the length of the route, the frequency of departures and sometimes the fee schedules can fluctuate. Some routes terminate in the late evening hours, before they reach their normal daytime end points.

You can catch private transportation at that time, as long as you are careful. Also be aware that bus drivers don't depart until the bus is almost full, so you may have to sit on the bus while the driver waits for sufficient people to get on board.

4. Accommodations

Luxury Hotels - $315 USD to $1050 USD & up

If you want to stay in the lap of luxury, you can do it for less in Cairo than in many other tourist meccas. You'll get all the extras at rates that aren't as high as you'd think.

Four Seasons Hotel Cairo Nile Plaza – $350 USD per night and up

This hotel is family-friendly and found in the center of town. It's less than a mile from the Egyptian Museum and Tahrir Square. The Cairo Tower and Coptic Museum are within two miles. The Four Seasons has a full-service guest spa, two outdoor pools and five restaurants.

The Nile Ritz Carlton - Cairo - $330 USD per night and up

The Ritz Carlton is a luxury hotel located at the heart of the city, within a 15 minute walk of the League of Arab States and Tahrir Square. The Egyptian Museum is just over a half mile away. They offer a full-service spa, four restaurants, a health club, five bars and an outdoor pool, all onsite.

JW Marriott Hotel Cairo - $315 USD per night and up

You'll find the JW Marriott in New Cairo City, about 16 miles from Cairo International Stadium, the Egyptian Presidential Palace and the International Convention Center. It offers guests a spa, 11 restaurants and two outdoor pools, along with free shuttle service to and from the airport.

Mid-Range Hotels in Cairo - $150 USD to $300 USD per night and up

If you're more interested in visiting as many places as possible, you can save money with a mid-priced hotel. They still have some of the same amenities found in the higher priced hotels.

Fairmont Towers – $175 USD per night and up

This luxury resort is in Heliopolis, within six miles of the convention center and stadium. It boasts numerous restaurants, a 24/7 casino and three outdoor pools. They have a free shuttle for shoppers, along with a poolside bar, two lounges and a health club.

Dusit Thani LakeView Cairo – $207 USD per night and up

This family-friendly hotel is located in New Cairo City. It's just a bit over 11 miles from the convention center and 12 miles from Cairo

International Stadium. It features a nightclub, full-service spa and a restaurant. They have a free airport shuttle, a health club and a bar/lounge.

Royal Maxim Palace Kempinski Cairo – $180 USD per night and up

New Cairo City is the home for this family-friendly hotel. It's about 12 miles from Cairo International Stadium and Cairo International Convention Center. They offer eight restaurants, an indoor pool and a full-service spa. You'll also find two bars, an outdoor pool and a night club on-site.

Cairo Hotels for the Budget-Conscious – $50-$140 USD per night

You don't have to break the bank to spend a few days in Cairo. These budget-friendly hotels are comfortable if not lavish, and have impressive amenities for their price range.

Tolip El Galaa Cairo Hotel – $67 USD per night and up

This economically priced luxury hotel in Heliopolis is just over two miles from City Stars Shopping and six miles from the Egyptian Presidential Palace, Cairo International Convention Center and Cairo International Stadium. They offer all smoke-free rooms, a full-service spa and two outdoor pools. Also on-site, you'll find a poolside bar, a bar/lounge and a health club.

The Oasis Hotel Pyramids – $55 USD per night and up

This lovely spa hotel is located in Giza. They're just nine miles from the Sphinx and Pyramids of Giza. Within 10 miles, you'll find the Orman Botanical Gardens and Dream Park. They offer a full-service spa, two restaurants and free buffet breakfast, along with an outdoor pool, bar/lounge, nightclub and a fitness center.

Concorde El Salam Hotel –$100 USD per night and up

The Concorde El Salam is found in the elegant suburb of Heliopolis. It's just a 10-minute ride from the airport and about a half hour's ride from the downtown area. The Egyptian Museum is only nine miles away. Their outdoor pool is surrounded with lush gardens, and they even have an equestrian center and complimentary shuttle service to the airport.

Airbnb's

You can rent a private room with a bed in the center of Cairo for only $10 per night. It has a great view, and is close to many places of interest in Cairo. It's quiet, modern, air-conditioned and recently renovated, and 10 minutes or less to all the central Cairo districts. It also comes with free Wi-Fi and a smart TV.

On the other end of the price scale is a $249 per night upscale 22nd floor apartment in Cairo.

The views are of the panoramic Cairo skyline and the majestic Nile River. The apartment is furnished beautifully and just minutes from famous historical sites in Cairo, along with many restaurants.

Airbnb also has spacious sites that can hold up to 16 people, at higher prices. There are currently 279 Cairo rentals available on Airbnb.com.

5. Sightseeing

It's hard to suggest where to head first when you arrive in Cairo with your heart set on sightseeing. The most obvious and highly popular locations are the Giza Sphinx and the Pyramids at Giza. These are among the seven wonders of the ancient world, and well worth the visit.

You may also enjoy Khan al-Khalili, which is a bustling market that allows you to experience the bazaar of Cairo as it was over 500 years ago. Old Cairo is also popular among visitors. It is an ancient Coptic Christian community that dates back to Roman times.

Other favorite historic sites in or near Cairo include the Saladin Citadel with its stunning mosques, and the ancient Hanging Church. Don't discount the local museums. They are among the world's most impressive, including the Egyptian Museum of Antiquities.

The Giza Pyramid Complex

The pyramids of Giza complex is the famous archeological site in Egypt, found just outside Cairo. The Great Pyramids are among the best known structures in the world. The Great Sphinx is a wondrous, massive structure that is known worldwide. The pyramids symbolize ancient Egypt in the imagination of the Western world. The Great Pyramid is the only one of seven ancient wonders of the world still in existence.

The Mosque of Muhammad Ali at the Citadel

This may not be the oldest Cairo mosque, but it has a grandeur that's hard to top. It's likely the most popular of the area's Islamic mosques for tourists. It is sometimes called the Alabaster Mosque, since that stone was used extensively on the outside walls and some other surfaces.

The Hanging Church

This historic church is sometimes called the Suspended Church. Layers of stones and logs of trees were built atop ruins of a Roman fort, for use as a foundation. The wooden roof was made in the shape of Noah's Ark.

The Hanging Church was the residence of the Coptic Patriarch from the 7th to 13th century. It has also been the site of important religious ceremonies and elections.

Tahrir Square Historic & Revolution Site

Also called Martyr Square and Liberation Square, this is the major downtown square of Cairo. It was the focus and location for political demonstrations, particularly those leading to the revolution and resignation of then-President Hosni Mubarak in 2011.

Around the square are other historic sites, including the Kasr El Dobara Evangelical Church, the Arab League headquarters, the Mogamma government building, the House of Folklore and the Egyptian Museum.

Khan al-Khalili Marketplace

This impressive marketplace has shops arranged around small sized courtyards. It's like a historic mini-mall, where vendors sell everything from tourist trinkets to semi-precious stones to soap.

The khan was once divided fairly rigidly, but the only truly separate districts now are those of the spice dealers, gold sellers and coppersmiths. The merchants here are notoriously smooth-talking. You can buy almost anything here, and if you're looking for something specific and one merchant doesn't carry it, he'll find another shopkeeper who does.

6. Eat & Drink

The cuisine of Egypt is largely dependent on legumes like lentils and beans, in addition to vegetables, which appear in most Egyptian dishes. Pasta and rice are used in some dishes, and many dishes include sauces that offer truly unique tastes.

Aish, an Egyptian bread, forms part of most meals. In Egyptian, this word means bread, and it means life, as well. If you don't have cutlery on your table, you may use the bread for your food, where you would normally use a fork or spoon.

Kushari is often cited as the national dish of Egypt, but in fact it was brought to Egypt by British army chefs in the 19th century.

The Cairo restaurants in our guide are classified into three price points:

Expensive Prices ($50 USD $100 USD)
Moderate Prices ($25 USD to $50 USD)
Inexpensive Prices (under $25 USD)

Abou el-Sid – Expensive

Abou el-Sid is a favorite restaurant for locals and tourists alike, who want authentic Egyptian food. It offers a warm atmosphere as a backdrop for some delicious Egyptian dishes, including their Circasian Chicken in Walnut Sauce and Stuffed Pigeon with Rice or Frik (cereal food made with green wheat).

Birdcage - Expensive

This restaurant has a welcoming atmosphere and a beautiful interior. The waiters are happy to suggest delicious dishes. A few of the favorites served here include shrimp curry, phad thai and chicken green curry.

The Grill Restaurant & Lounge– Expensive

From the lovely views of the Nile to the friendly staff and tasteful food, this restaurant is one that's worth a visit. The staff are helpful and cheerful, and the menu has delectable items including rib eye and salmon steak.

Moderately Priced Restaurants

Night & Day Restaurant - Moderate

The name of this restaurant describes the meals they serve. Their buffet breakfast is available daily, with pastries, cakes, salads and fresh fruits. With a view of the Nile, you'll enjoy a delicious lunch or dinner, too. A few of the favorites here are Veal Scallop, Spaghetti Bolognaise and Pan-Fried Sea Bass Harrah Style.

Osmanly Restaurant – Moderate

This restaurant has several menu items that are consistently popular with expats and visitors alike. From lentil soup and breaded cheese to tagines with couscous, there are no boring dishes. The most popular dish is likely the Chef mezzas selection of nine samples, each one a delicious appetizer. If you have room, try their pudding and fresh fruit dessert.

Loft 21 - Moderate

This is a wonderfully relaxing and elegant place to eat, whether you visit in the daytime or at night. The wait staff is attentive and the food is hard to beat. Some of the favorites include sea bass filet, lamb shank, roast broccoli with garlic oil and goat cheese and hazelnut salad.

Inexpensive Cairo Restaurants

Bab El Sharq – Inexpensive

It's hard to find really good service at many Cairo restaurants, but this place does it, according to people who have eaten here. They have wonderful appetizers like Mombar and Cheese Sambousek. Popular entrees include Penne Arabiata, Chinese Shrimp and Oriental Molokhia Chicken.

Sequoia – Inexpensive

Many first-time visitors take locals' suggestions to visit this restaurant for an inexpensive treat. The view and service are exceptional, and it is often recommended. Some of their popular entrees include Fatta Chicken Shawerma, Garlic Roasted Potatoes with Meat Tagen and Quails Marinated in Pomegranate Syrup.

Taboula Lebanese Restaurant – Inexpensive

Walking down steps and out of the hot sun, you'll find yourself in Taboula. It's old fashioned and elegant, with exotic lighting and colorful trays. Visitors love the large portions and delectable foods. Some of the favorites include kofka, vine leaves, taboule and hommos.

7. Culture and Entertainment

The legacy of Cairo spans millennia, even though it was only built in its present form just over 1000 years ago. It is a monument to an empire that was once the longest lived of its time.

Cairo has almost seven million residents, and it is among the most densely populated cities in the world. It's a cosmopolitan city, which incorporates elements from many cultures, along with those of its past.

The area where Cairo was built was once home to great Ancient Egyptian cities, and its cultural, historical sites include the Sphinx and Pyramids of Giza.

Beit El-Umma Museum

This "House of the People" was built in the 1800s as a residence for Saad Zaghlul, the Wafd party founder and at the time the nationalist leader for modern Egypt. A bronze statue of

Saad Zaghlul (1857-1927) marks its entrance. It has been preserved carefully in its original form as a museum that provides visitors with a look inside the lives of 1800s-1900s political elites and their lifestyles.

Beshtak Palace

This is a favorite tourist spot, since the museum documents Cairo's history as a city. The exterior was built in 1334, and shows unusual screened windows. The second floor has painted wood and gilt paneling, pointed arches and stained glass windows, which set it apart from most other buildings of the same era.

Abdeen Palace

This is a famous palace built during Mohamed Ali Pasha reign. It served as seat for the Egyptian government from 1872 until 1952. The palace complex has a museum of military arms that were presented to former President Mubarak as gifts. It includes medals bestowed on the members of the royal family of Egypt and eminent figures in the country.

Cairo Entertainment

In addition to the many historic monuments and structures in the Cairo area, it's also home to plenty of places that will entertain your family or friends. Cairo is about history, but it also has a firm grasp on the present and the future, in the world of entertainment.

Giza Pharonic Family Village

This village is a popular tourist attraction that offers a good time for everyone in your family, with the children being targeted specifically for fun. It's an ancient theme park on the west bank of the Nile. As a visitor, you'll ride in a small boat through reed beds, while costumed actors play out live scenes recreating daily Pharonic life.

Ballet & Opera Performances in Cairo

Many performances take place each year in the Opera house of Cairo. Dance troops and companies visit the city to faithfully present their art. You will find some performances at the Gomhyrya theatre, as well.

The Egyptian Culture Ministry holds a huge production of "Aida", which was written to honor the Suez Canal opening. Some of the previous performances were held in Karnack temple in Luxor and the temple Hatshepsut, and the last venue for the opera was in the Giza pyramid complex.

Belly Dancing

Oriental dancing is something tourists in Egypt love to see. The art goes back to the Pharaoh's times. Many of the tombs and temples of the Pharaohs have drawings that clarify the importance of belly dancing in the ancient Egyptian celebrations and rituals.

Cairo Night-life

Like other great cities, Cairo comes alive after dark. A delicious and vibrant blend of sounds and sights begins taking shape as the sun sets. It showcases the glittering vistas of the city, the music's pulse and colored lights showing from Nile-floating boats.

Even though the city is mainly Islamic, there are many bars for tourists. In Cairo, you'll find the busiest night spots downtown and in the Mohandeseen and Zamalek neighborhoods.

Cairo Casinos

Many of the casinos in Cairo's 5-star hotels are open to all except Egyptians. You'll have to show your passport at the door. The games are conducted in US dollars and other foreign currencies. Smart casual is the dress code. Cairo hotels that have casinos include the Marriott and Semiramis Intercontinental.

After Eight Club

The philosophy of the After Eight Club is music – more specifically, underground, Oriental music. It represents their culture, and their bands cover all types of tastes. They have a relaxed atmosphere, and expect only positive interactions of their guests, regardless of their gender, culture, age or sexual nature. They ask only that you enjoy their music and respect everyone's fun.

Graffiti Bar & Lounge

This is the newest, hottest Cairo lounge. They offer flavor and freshness, with abundant entertainment, which includes art installations, stand-up comedians, guest DJs and live bands. Fun is the word of the night and there is something for everyone.

8. Special Events in Cairo

There is always something interesting going on in Cairo, and we'll describe some of the most notable events below.

January

Coptic Christmas
This is held in the first days of January, with many celebrations that include festive music, colorful parades and dancing. You can see them in Cairo's Coptic Quarter in December, as well as January in pre and post-Christmas revelry.

March

Coptic Easter
During this festival, people visit family members and partake of huge feasts. It's not all fun, though – church-goers also faithfully attend services.

April

Shem al Nessim

This name translates roughly to "first day of the new spring". It is celebrated on the first Monday that falls after Coptic Easter. It is a national holiday. Lots of families enjoy picnics and other activities out of doors.

June

Evacuation Day

This holiday marks the Republic's declaration in 1953, and the foreign troop removal in 1956.

July

Revolution Day

This holiday is celebrated throughout Egypt, marking the anniversary of Egyptian's royal government's fall and the 1952 rise of the Egyptian Republic.

August

Cairo International Song Festival

This is held at a variety of locations in Cairo, celebrating music, singers and songwriters. It is done in tribute to international stars who have impacted the music world in a major way. The festival also holds a major competition for international performers.

October

Armed Forces Day

The Egyptian forces crossed the Suez Canal in 1973, during their war with Israel. Anwar Sadat was assassinated in 1981, while watching the parade marking this day. This holiday commemorates both of these events.

November

Arabic Music Festival

This festival is held each year at the Cairo Opera House. It celebrates Arabic music's long tradition. They invite leading singers and musicians, along with ensembles, to perform for all the listeners.

December

The Cairo International Film Festival

This festival, held annually, hosts previews of obscure worldwide film offerings. It is in its 26th year, and was the first film festival of its type to be held in the Middle East.

Religious Festivals

The main festivals in the Muslim religion are Ramadan and Eid al-Fitr. The Islamic calendar is followed in setting the dates, so they fall one month earlier every year.

Ramadan

This is a Muslim religious festival that lasts for a month. During the period, the devout Muslims will allow nothing past their lips, like drink or food, as long as the sky is light. After sunset, and before sunrise, they hold massive feasts.

Offices and shops have erratic schedules during this time. People may sleep in the afternoon. It is impolite to drink or eat in any public place while they are fasting, so tourists should use discretion, even though you won't be expected to observe Ramadan yourself. Hotels for tourists are not usually affected, but some restaurants close down for the full month.

Eid al-Fitr

This marks the end of the month of Ramadan. Muslims will feast for three days, slaughtering goats and sheep. Some residents will leave the city to visit family and friends, but the city is still noisy, due to the animals awaiting their fate in pens beside the streets. If you're sensitive to the welfare of animals, you may not want to be in the city during this holiday.

9. Safety in Cairo

You can walk safely around most main Cairo streets any time you like. It is usually fairly safe, and there are always many people smiling and asking if you need help. If you're female, however, you should expect to be targeted with catcalling.

In touristy areas, there are more helpful people around. Don't go with anyone you don't know or allow anyone to guide or push you anywhere you don't want to be. If you wander too far and become lost, look around for police and security officers. Many of them speak at least a little English, and they know the area well, if you have questions.

Crossing the streets of Cairo is challenging. Traffic lights are largely non-existent, and even where there are signals, they are usually ignored by drivers. Police officers sometimes control traffic during the busiest times.

Crossing the street involves hurrying past the lanes one at a time, whenever there is a traffic break. If all else fails, stand next to a native Egyptian who is going to cross the street and follow him closely.

Taxi drivers sometimes drive erratically or fast. If you don't feel safe in a cab, inform the driver to stop and then get out of the vehicle.

10. Conclusion

Cairo has always attracted travelers, even 10 centuries ago. The enchanting, surprising, crowded, hectic, beautiful city is still "The City Victorious", as the Egyptians call it, or "Masr", which is also the name for Egypt.

Cairo is among the largest urban areas in the world, and there are many things to see. You won't want to leave without heading to the Great Pyramids of Giza. You'll also find Egyptian Antiquities Museums, Muslim monuments, Christian churches and ancient tombs and temples.

If you allow your senses to wander, you can lose yourself within this majestic city. You'll discover the sweetness that is Cairo, the pleasure of strolling down its narrow streets and the warmth and friendliness of small, local cafes. You could describe Cairo in many different ways, but there is no ONE way to discover what you'll experience here. The city is one of a kind.

Cairo is filled with movement and life, nearly 24 hours each day. The children play in the streets and the many drivers honk their horns on busy thoroughfares. Merchants sell their services and wares, and as a backdrop to it all, you see the majesty of the Great Pyramid. Visiting Cairo is an experience you will never forget.

Made in the USA
Lexington, KY
24 September 2018